A Few of

ALSO BY GEORGE BRADLEY

POETRY

Terms to Be Met (1986)
Of the Knowledge of Good and Evil (1991)
The Fire Fetched Down (1996)
Some Assembly Required (2001)

AS EDITOR

The Yale Younger Poets Anthology (1998)

A Few of Her Secrets

George Bradley

WAYWISER

First published in 2011 by

THE WAYWISER PRESS

Bench House, 82 London Road, Chipping Norton, Oxon OX7 5FN, UK
P.O. Box 6205, Baltimore, MD 21206, USA
http://waywiser-press.com

Editor-in-Chief
Philip Hoy

Senior American Editor
Joseph Harrison

Associate Editors
Clive Watkins   Greg Williamson

Cover image:

Copyright © George Bradley, 2011

The right of George Bradley to be identified as the author of this work
has been asserted by him in accordance with the
Copyright, Designs and Patents Act of 1988.

All rights reserved

A CIP catalogue record for this book is available from the British Library

ISBN 978-1-904130-42-0

Printed and bound by
T.J. International Ltd., Padstow, Cornwall, PL28 8RW

Acknowledgements

The following poems first appeared in the following publications:

Denver Quarterly: "The Way Antelope Used to Be"
Literary Imagination: "Village Romance"
New England Review: "The Serpent's Seed"
The New Criterion: "The kiss of death"
The Paris Review: "Advisory," "A Few of Her Secrets," "The Future of the Past"
Poetry: "Liturgy"
Southwest Review: "Elixir"
Standpoint (UK): "Based on a True Story," "*Coup de Vieux*"
The Yale Review: "Life and Death Matters"

"Gathered from *The Tempest*" first appeared as a broadside published by The Acre (Andover, Massachusetts) and printed by Bull Thistle Press.

"*La pastasciutta con quello che c'è*" first appeared in *Sustenance & Desire*, an anthology featuring the paintings of Bascove and published by David R. Godine.

"Gathered from *The Tempest*," "*La pastasciutta con quello che c'è*," and "Problems in Carolingian Art" also appeared in *Under the Rock Umbrella*, an anthology published by Mercer University Press.

"Advisory" also appeared in *Poetry Calendar 2007*, published by Alhambra Publishers, as the poem for September 11th.

"Glass Door" first appeared in *Poetry Calendar 2008*, published by Alhambra Publishers.

LEEDS LIBRARIES AND INFORMATION SERVICE	
LD 4265157 3	
ASKEWS & HOLT	04-Apr-2011
811.5	£8.99
S035179	

Contents

Gathered from *The Tempest*   9

I

Limit	13
The Serpent's Seed	14
A Few of Her Secrets	16
Advisory	17
Based on a True Story	18
Sette Ricette	19
1. *Arista di maiale*	19
2. *Tagliata di manzo con rucola*	19
3. *Bistecche di vitello come tordi*	20
4. *Pollo alla cacciatora*	20
5. *La fettunta*	21
6. *Coniglio al forno*	21
7. *La pastasciutta con quello che c'è*	22
Elixir	23
In the Garden of Fine Kurdish Weaving	24
The Way Antelope Used to Be	26
The Two Economies	28
My Twentieth Century Europe	30
Kulturträger	31
The kiss of death	32
The Itinerary	33
The Attic	34

II

Glass Door	37
Village Romance	38
Lonesome Booze Blues	39
Schlimmbesserung	41

Contents

Teaching the Controversy	43
Response	44
Event Horizon	46
Problems in Carolingian Art	47
De Monumentis	49
Entry Level Elective	51
What It Takes	52
The Future of the Past	54
The Decline of the Western	56
The Prophet Joel on the Division of Labor	58
Coup de Vieux	59
Liturgy	61
Life and Death Matters	63
A Note About George Bradley	67

Gathered from *The Tempest*

for Richard Howard

Art's an island in the storm,
And under its instructive spell,
Those cast up there cannot know
How much the harmony and form
Plucked from the air by Ariel
Was first prepared by Prospero.

I

Limit

Beast put to pasture does not feed
At ease, but battens to the fence,
Describing the circumference
Of opportunity and need;
Grazing best pushes to where
An eager tooth can only nibble,
Seeking beyond close-cropped stubble
Scents so sharp the nostrils flare.

The Serpent's Seed

Walking into the world they were not afraid
at first, though they had every right to be:
they were young and inexperienced – by some
calculations no more than a few hours old –
and it had already been a difficult day.
In spite of interrogation and catastrophe
and a contact with divinity that set the tone
for the fall of Jerusalem and the resurrection
of blood libel and all manner of numinous
hap, they were thinking of other things.
They had recently engaged in intercourse,
and he was curious how long it might take
her to become interested in the act again;
she wondered when she could once more fall
asleep. They had eaten forbidden fruit,
and she was thinking how that lapse
had worked, that she was his equal now
and not subservient to him as he to God;
but this was not what the man was thinking.
He thought she, too, looked capable of sweat.
So in their solitary way, their minds were full,
and they had not yet made a place for fear.
The thing God called death and the angel
had emphasized, brandishing gladiate fire,
remained an abstraction still, and the horns
and talons and tusks and other snakes
they would meet – the *boomslang* set to drop
from trees they stopped beneath for shade;
the *shushupe*, twelve gracile feet and aggressive –
did not occasion any particular concern.
The man thought that was what sticks were for,
the woman that was why she accepted the man.
Not Behemoth, his bones like bars of iron,
not Leviathan, that maketh the deep to boil,
nothing that swam or crawled or flew

The Serpent's Seed

disheartened them, though the darkness came,
and an incidental violence gave out its cry.
Who had now the angel's example of flame
and thereby a stratagem, had also the labor
as distraction inherent in God's sentence,
they had not had leisure to recall, and hence
hand in hand on the subjected plain they took
it with them unawares, their fateful freight,
bearing its planted seed as she now carried his,
an afterthought that would flower over time
into mayhem and various standards of beauty,
into mutual distrust and a more-than-feral
cunning: the trepidation born of regret, which
is what the serpent knew and gave to them
and they brought out of Eden to this earth.

A Few of Her Secrets

No one knew her real name, but she appeared to be Greek.
She posed nude for painters, when she could find them.
She could slap hard enough to draw blood.
She slept around.
She was not one of those women who behave like cats, jumping into your lap when you sit down to read.
Ignore her, and she ignored you.
Yet she was jealous. She would wound.
She dressed in classical rags, shawls and hobble skirts, the shot-silk cloak and snood.
She spoke many languages and was not interested in disguising her intelligence.
Incense-laden atmosphere drove her wild. She loved the pagan remains of festivals and insisted on visiting cathedrals.
Although she had no compunction about lying, as a character witness she was useless: she had substance-abuse problems and no known address.
She claimed to be the most attractive woman of Greek extraction in the world, but in truth she was not pretty in a conventional way. Her beauty was in the beholding.
The objects of her affection seemed unsatisfactory. She gave herself to real pigs, neurasthenic little boys, epicene aesthetes.
Faithful only to the dead, she kept private anniversaries, weeping quietly in the small hours.
She was generous. She could not be embarrassed or intimidated or bought.
She was not to be relied on for anything. She made an inconvenient neighbor.
She was always the older woman.
She did not leave notes when she left.

Advisory

for Jim Kehoe

September's lovely in New York, the sky
Returned to baby blue, the breeze now mild
As breath, and if you've anything at all
Important planned, now's when to do it: fall
In love, begin a book, beget a child,
Marry, get religion, learn to fly.

September's stunning, even on so odd
An island as Manhattan, of all places
Least like landscape: climate cannot bungle
This month without a more than urban jungle,
Without an icecap, or those desert spaces
Composed of dust and emptiness and God.

September's drop-dead gorgeous or it's plain
Disaster here, airborne catastrophe,
Some sub-tropical depression, say,
Originating half a world away
And gaining, as it moves across the sea,
The turbine fury of a hurricane.

Still, September's dangerous days are few,
Whirlwinds tracked worldwide. You can assume
Responsible officials will foresee
Such turmoil; you can count on your TV
For early warning. There are those for whom
This hasn't worked, but it should work for you.

I know a man who paused to say goodbye
With care to those he loved one morning, fold
Them in his arms, and just that slight delay
Spared him on a bright September day
When air turned ash, the center could not hold,
The quickly dead fell burning from the sky.

Based on a True Story

No, not equal to, not ever, for all
it couples in public vehicles and crawls
through sewers as through astonishing bars
of light, of music, but rather a bizarre
bazaar of retailed wisdom and aperçu
happily assembled out of what you
will, so that it variously contains
a woman, a bed, wind and rain,
heaven and hell, a mouse's nest,
a winter's midnight dressed
in radiant bolts of shimmer shots,
its construct *ad hoc* on its base yet not
the thing itself, being for better and worse
a derivation, a version and perverse.
Put much in and most is left
over, the sprawled magnitude of evasion deft.
Leave everything out and some trace
inheres in what sparse space
affords. Pare it down, puff
it up, it cannot be pruned or plumped enough
to be coterminous with its occasion, but must extend
elsewhere, more rational and pointed, to an end
and to our eyes
more moving. More shapely. More concise.

Sette Ricette

1. *Arista di maiale*

When buying loin of pork, first satisfy
Yourself that it is flexible and tender.
Ask for the ribs to be removed, but keep
A layer of fat for flavor. Wash and dry
The meat and make many incisions; render
Them larger with your fingers, pushing deep
Into but not through the flesh; then heap
The holes with salt, and press a quarter clove
Of garlic into each, plus fresh rosemary.
Sear the meat in good oil on the stove,
Cook in the oven till it meets a fork
Firmly, say an hour, and now your work
Is done. "Arista" comes from Greek, "the very
Best." This is the best way to cook pork.

2. *Tagliata di manzo con rucola*

Rinse some fresh arrugula of grit,
Dry it, chop it, then set it aside
And grill a T-bone steak that's spent a bit
Of time in wine. When it approaches rare,
Slice the meat onto enamel ware,
Dress it in olive oil emulsified
With lemon juice, plus salt and pepper, pass
Under flame again for warmth and color,
Add the arrugula, and it's complete.
Omnivores, ready to eat a bull or
Something that the bull itself might eat,
We humans are in a dietary class
By ourselves, as this dish will attest:
The greens lend spice and help us to digest.

Sette Ricette

3. *Bistecche di vitello come tordi*

Salt some veal chops lightly (this receipt
Has salt to spare) and brown them in a pan.
Add sage and garlic, lowering the heat,
Since both these have a tendency to burn;
Then pour in wine, plus chicken stock to cover,
And braise the chops for twenty minutes. Turn
Them frequently, for veal is lean and can
Easily dry out. When almost through
Add diced *prosciutto* (any ham will do,
But it's the makings make the cook). Reduce
The liquid to a sauce and serve it over
The dish. This is a method once in use
For *tordo*, a delicious little thrush
Now met in Horace more than in the bush.

4. *Pollo alla cacciatora*

The means Italian hunters use to mask
The heavy taste of game have here instead
Been given the unenviable task
Of flavoring insipid poultry bred
On factory farms polluting Arkansas:
Place chicken pieces in a casserole,
Season them, and fry them in some oil
With bay leaves and black olives till the raw
Look disappears; add plum tomatoes, whole
Garlic cloves, sliced onions, and red wine;
Cover the chicken loosely with some foil,
Bake it in the oven, and you'll dine
Delectably within the hour. One could
Cook cardboard in this way and find it good.

Sette Ricette

5. *La fettunta*

The simple yet nutritious food with which
Italian peasants once addressed their wants
Is lately all the rage in restaurants
Around the world that cater to the rich,
Serving humble fare at any price.
Take what Tuscans call "the oily slice":
Day-old bread grilled on an open fire,
Cleaned up where it was burnt a bit on purpose,
Then rubbed with garlic while the toast is warm
Until a full clove melts into its surface,
And soaked in olive oil that's freshly pressed.
If the bread lacks salt, as is the norm
In Tuscany, add salt as you require.
The oil's the point, so you should use the best.

6. *Coniglio al forno*

There is an ideal world, as dreamt by Plato,
And then there is the world that we inhabit
In which we're understeeled and overfed
And cannot bring ourselves to raise a rabbit,
Cut its throat, suspend the corpse to drain
Of blood, behead it, gut and skin it, hack
It up.... Best buy your bunny ready-slain
And sectioned; place the pieces on a bed
Of carrot, fennel leaf, and sliced potato,
With olive oil and salt; now roast and baste
The dish till meat falls from the bone. It's true,
Rabbit retains a gamy aftertaste
Regardless, but it's nothing like the smack
Of hunted hare, more suited to a stew.

Sette Ricette

7. *La pastasciutta con quello che c'è*

The thing about dried pasta is, it waits
Until you want it and provides a plan
Where one was lacking. Nothing but a can
Of beets left in the house? Then improvise
An onion and a touch of cream, and if
You've got *farfalle*, you've got "Pink Bow Ties."
(No cream at all? It's "Bloody Butterflies.")
Left-over anchovies and just a whiff
Of garlic is the best that you can do?
Tossing them with olive oil creates
A classic, if you have *fusilli*, too.
Dried pasta's how a cook accommodates
The facts. No artist makes the most of his
Dreams who can't make much of what there is.

Elixir

Of what virtue is it composed?
> Splinters of conscience and the ash of youth; fish-tails left in the sun; the bones of mice; insult; worms.

By what process does it form?
> Time and pressure yield its fossil fuel, this liquid seeping.

To what use might it be put?
> It shall animate interaction like hot punch; it shall stoke great striving; of bitter amplitude, it shall be sustenance when much else lacks.

How is it given to be abused?
> It may be one thirst at the expense of others; it can scar; it is explosive, dangerous in unskilled hands.

What will be left when it drains?
> It does not drain.

What is to be done as its accumulates?
> It is to be dammed and bridged or to be disguised. It is to swallow down or mop up.

How is its excess to be discarded?
> Pour it over corpses at the hour of death, the quicklime in each coffin. Let its vitriol, that flensed fat, strip away flesh like illusion.

Who will inherit its asperity?
> Those strong enough for rapture, dewy-eyed endurers. It shall be felt within them as desire, who aim at its possession, who hope by bearing to bear it on.

How will they absorb its gift?
> It shall be brought to their lips in a beaker of pain, its odor an acrid incense, its flowing something like water, its look the look of flame.

How may its recipients be known?
> They persist, stony in failure, unmollified by success. They perturb. Long after sane motivation comes to rest, their words unsettle. They astonish, that their transport be akin to rage and their animus devotion in itself.

In the Garden of Fine Kurdish Weaving

*"Where the Arab sets his foot, the grass
will never grow again"* the saying runs,
and in northeast Iraq's debated land
of Kurdistan, tempting as any garden,
Arab raiders have come countless times
to slaughter the inhabitants like sheep,

burn encampments, drive horse and sheep
down to the plains below. And yet the grass
of the Zagros mountains recovers time
and again, fed by deep snows that run
out of ravines in spring to water gardens
some emir ordains in a distant land,

and when the heat first grips the table land
to wither winter's bloom, a nomad's sheep
must be transhumed. Abandoning truck gardens
and rude huts for an altitude where grass
survives in summer, bands of migrants run
their flocks along a route established time

out of mind. A season's change is time
for rural chores in this relentless land,
where custom rules and obligation runs
deep as blood, and now the fat-tailed sheep
are shorn, since sheep are how a season's grass
becomes the carded substance of a garden

carpet, yarn to fabricate the Garden
of Eden some place in these hills in time
elapsed. Children pick burs and bits of grass
out of the wool, and men use what the land
affords as stain to saturate the sheep-
white skeins, letting the excess dyestuff run

In the Garden of Fine Kurdish Weaving

off in the hardwater streams that run
through Kurdistan. Then women weave the garden –
trees and fountains, birds and fish and sheep –
an ideal place imagined out of time
and walled off by a border stripe from land
where life is transience and flesh is grass.

Khans decide the grass and claim to run
the land, but any Kurd may own a garden
given time and care, the stuff of sheep.

The Way Antelope Used to Be

Home on the range, we had trouble with nostalgia,
though everything had been changing furiously
for as long as anyone could remember, and each
of us was constitutionally guaranteed the right
to distort the accumulation in his own way.

Still, no one had any training in perspective,
and our far-flung places imitated one another
in their utilitarian architecture and innocent
dementia. The ax-maniac down at the TireTown
told everybody to take care. Then he slashed
all the tires. Bleeding, this incident introduced
the Evening News, and a few of us filed it away
for later recall, when the great wave of the future
receded and that year's version of distant famine
had been retrofitted with another catastrophe.

Alas, our heap of recollection did not climb high.
We had small past to break out anywhere,
nor hearts prepared for bursting, and viewed
our lives from the windows of automobiles, waiting
to rubberneck the pile-up when our turn came.
With no inheritance in dispute except as catalogued
and no form of oral history not to be discounted,
our grandmothers struggled to quantify
the effects of a fungible aphasia, and where
amid such *ad hoc* drift was one to locate joy?

Luckily, longing proved more gifted than any
of us, the innate tenderness steady in its appeal;
happily our elders were resilient and ready
to imagine extra hard. Tottering across factory
farms and through the gates of National Parks,
they swaddled the bare facts in diaphanous
invention, decorating empty acres with the gilt

The Way Antelope Used to Be

of human desire, the pristine dream of dawn
forced once to gleam and glinting to be gone.

The Two Economies

They had breakfast meetings and conference calls and weekly brainstorming sessions.
Our brains stormed in private.

They moved into corner offices and were entitled to executive suites.
We had a view of the rooftops of Queens.

They were heavily credentialed. They wore identities around their necks and emotions on their sleeves.
We recognized one another as dogs do, by sniffing.

They commuted in vehicles that cost as much as small houses. They slumbered in stretch limousines.
We slept in cars too.

They attended recruitment fairs and job seminars and annual sales conventions.
We met warily. We were unconventional.

They marketed to target audiences, operating on the basis of focus groups and statistically significant samples.
We never knew our audience. We danced in small spotlights, one lap at a time.

Messages arrived for them at inconvenient moments, and they were obliged to excuse themselves.
We understood.

They built custom homes and bought plots in the best cemeteries.
We were buried in books.

They dreamed of writing novels in gorgeous locales after their hangovers wore off.
So did we, and sometimes wrote them.

The Two Economies

They were well compensated. Their emoluments were calculated
 as a percentage of return.
We distressed ourselves for a song.

They knew obscenity when they saw it, and they saw it often. They
 knew what they liked and saved the receipt.
We knew solitude. We knew obsession. We knew joy.

My Twentieth Century Europe

As many people know and a few still remember,
for most of the twentieth century the irregular peninsula
referred to as Europe was not a very good place to be.
> *Sometimes a blanket of fire falls out of the sky*
> *Periodically stone comes undone as cathedrals collapse*
> *Now and then every boy in the village is taken off and shot*

Invasion, genocide, revolution, civil war: usual
and unusual versions of Armageddon reigned, relieved
by intervals of social engineering and widespread surveillance.

Europe, of course, is a privileged place, and elsewhere
in what used to be called the developing world,
conditions in the twentieth century were if anything worse.
> *Detached extremities line the banks of fever-afflicted rivers*
> *Migrant skeletons extend starvation over a clay craquelure*
> *Reeducated minds finally open to the twisted logic of vines*

Somehow the English-speaking world was often spared, was lucky,
and my North America has been so fortunate one has to laugh
when inhabitants voice their entirely unexceptional complaints.

To return to Europe, in the twentieth century it was a disaster,
though not a disaster for me, who experienced what remained
of its venerable culture while losing my hangover in sidewalk cafés.
> *I look for a waiter and order an americano at last*
> *I glance at a newspaper and try to think about soccer*
> *I spot an unfamiliar girl and contemplate a flirtation*

Around me, old people with the past in their eyes mourned
departed relatives and extinguished beliefs, but I felt no pity,
being young and unobservant and bound to catch up in time.

Kulturträger

Where there stretched open steppe, grassland
fat with blood, dark with sun-obscuring clouds
of arrows, we brought our disposition to cities,
our instinct for gardens and maintained walls.
(The black earth swallowed our crenelations;
bone-tipped projectiles did much execution.)

Where there was only erosion, bare skeletons
of rock and sudden storms of obliterating sand,
we labored to establish monasteries, desert islands
composed of ceremony and illuminated parchment.
(The waste submerged each ritual foundation;
eremites withered, the social monks declined.)

We constructed hospitals and houses of parliament
for fractious populations long afflicted by disease,
planned roads and universities, sanitary measures,
introduced crops and new techniques of cultivation.
(When we decamped, discouraged, all improvements
became caricatures, foolish ideas fallen into disuse.)

Ελληνικια, iuris-dictio, egalité, democratic values:
where there had been jungle, we cut clearings;
where there expanded ice, we circled up low huts;
where there was raw space, we built space stations.
(The vines returned, hutments lay buried in snow,
space junk yielded to gravity, dropping from the sky.)

And where there was nothing at all, no memory,
no accomplishment or distinction, no wit or will,
still we worked to locate ornament, imagined courts
and courtiers, robed attendants hovering in song.
(Lost legions destined for an unmarked grave, into
that barbaricum we marched, wave on civilizing wave.)

The kiss of death

rarely arrives with torches and the company
of soldiers. It is the true intimacy: private.
The kiss is not, as a rule, preceded
by forecast or preemptive forgiveness.
There exists no faith founded upon its reception.

The kiss of death is not given in haste.
It does not soar through the air on arrows,
does not pound positions on a battlefield,
does not rip through ribs on an assassin's knife.
Its violence is incremental, uneasily detected.

Nor is the kiss cold. It is not of marble
or of ice and does not thicken blood.
It asks no ghastliness to prompt its shiver.
Fresh as clean linen, delicate as your wrist,
it is felt in the slightest pressure, a caress.

The kiss is nothing if not subtle, and not
a few remain oblivious to its attentions:
they believe it to be cobwebs on their lips,
breezes in their hair, hair brushing brows.
They mistake it for sunlight on their skin.

Light as an eyelash, soft as thought,
the kiss is often missed, but some persist
in sensing their persistent familiar.
They grasp what spasm is prepared,
the greedy consummation that awaits.

There is a mortal rapture in all things.
The informed, the uninnocent, those
adequately versed, know every fear
is the same fear, and that its kiss
becomes us as the air we breathe.

The Itinerary

Some had to crawl there, some left on the run, some wandered off in the general direction.
Large numbers were scheduled to depart via major airports, where conditions remained taxing. Those left behind tried to work around the inconvenience.
Trains were old-fashioned, even cliché, but sufficed nonetheless.
Automobiles of every make proved extremely popular.
Some traveled weeping, some singing, some without paying attention.
Some journeyed in the company of multitudes, some were engaged in private expeditions.
The precocious were left to their own devices.
Not a few escaped jail.
It was not uncommon for lovers to walk out in the middle of trysts, abruptly abandoning significant others to the nuisance of cleaning up after.
A great many were wheeled away while occupying beds they did not own. The sheets needed changing, the soup on the tray was cold.
There were those who promised to look each other up once they got in, at which point they intended finally to get even.
Others vowed to have nothing to do with anyone ever again. Their absence was viewed as good riddance.
None quite believed the brochures. No one was happy about his ticket. Nobody liked the cost.
It was chaos and every agent's nightmare, but evidently the system worked. In retrospect there were no complaints.
They hurried, they hied, they made great haste.
They shuffled, they straggled, they sat right down and were dragged.
They were allowed to draw their own conclusions and did.
The sedentary often set out while in the bathroom.
Each improvisation was at last good enough, any individual enterprise was rewarded, and everybody was somehow satisfied in the end.
They arrived, feeling they had flown every step of the way.
They had all the time in the world.

The Attic

Some days on lazy afternoons it feels
as if nothing has ever changed and we
are children playing in the light that falls
across an attic floor. We brush away
cobwebs from old toys, try on discarded
clothes and costume jewelry, glance at letters
and books unread for years. We dig up hoarded
gold: discolored photos, hair that glitters
yet, the ringlets bright in rays inclined
to burnish each iota, mote, and smidgen
of dust disturbed while we content ourselves.
Below, adults who can't by now imagine
where we've gone will need to have explained
again how hours escape when time dissolves.

II

Glass Door

They'll risk a lot, the reckless adolescent,
intoxicated with the thought of flight
and lured to their dismay by vision's bright
idea. This autumn day, an April pheasant,
the tender skin beneath its wings all but
naked where the down had not yet grown
into its full-fledged glory, has just flown
out of the predatory air to what
seemed the refuge of an entrance way
to our garage and got its ring neck wrung,
sailing headlong into the unseen pane
and shattering the craning vertebrae
stretched in a race not to the swift or young
or innocent of light's legerdemain.

Village Romance

You were praying in the garden as usual, and damned
if the cup didn't pass, and what now? The discreet
leaves about your knees leapt into clarity as the sense
of things returned, flowed over you, its caress borne
as on a breeze – the odor of olives in bloom, the sound
of somebody snoring nearby, the buzz that testifies
to an interface with the busy hungers of this world –
and oh, in reprieve lies pleasure, surprise our precious
little joy, sing *hallelujah*, sing ally-in-come-free....
So in an access of delight the fizz seeped out,
and implication began to sink in. Come to think
of it, and a stay of execution isn't a bed of roses.
Lots of paperwork had to be filled out, and a mess
of details suddenly remained to be embraced, each
wanting the god squeezed out of it like lemon juice.
So many things left undone were now to do again.
For starters, all disciples must be told to take a bath.
Next, can the cook and upgrade the menu, because
there was no room in your new life for dried goat.
And then maybe you should throw a celebratory party,
invite the centurions and people you owed big-time
and anyone else you'd rather avoid, so that with the fun
wildly in progress, you might slip out a door and walk
through the neighborhood, trying to love it as of old,
before the ugly scenes, the unforgivable words;
of course, in rekindling the romance of circumstance,
the first move would be yours to make, for stone
is stolid stuff; but that wasn't out of the question,
at least not if night played its part, furnishing earth
with the definition of shadow, not if the weather
held, and dawn held off, and given the pinprick
of starlight to hold firmly against your eyes.

Lonesome Booze Blues

One thing you'll notice about your average opiate
of the masses is that it doesn't appreciate competition
from opium itself, nor from cigarettes and whiskey
and wild women, or any women at all, really, except
the kind of woman guaranteed to make you dream
of someone else, and while this seems counterintuitive,
at least from the point of view of attracting recruits,
such asceticism is age-old and not to be dismissed,
and what is it about starving or wearing barbed wire
or reading all of *Das Kapital* that makes people conceive
they have a leg up on sainthood, an edge on eternity?
After all, if heaven exists to be earned in abject
obeisance to command, gained in barter at the cost
of no deceiving, of no coveting your neighbor's ox
or ass, or his wife's ass for that matter, of no strong
language, no theft, no images even, then tell me
how is the sublime to take place, how will poetry
be possible, how can our obstinate angels believe
Paradise is worth the price of admission?

So do we console ourselves with a misnomer,
amusement our term for retreat. Yet if we swear
off irony, exfoliate the callus that facilitates evasion,
occasions of such avoidance remain, and what
about the significance of suffering, what about
the operation of sympathy in human response?
These are serious matters certainly and the stuff
of major literature, but probably the wrong
questions anyway, not that they don't deserve
answers, of which I invite you to take your pick:
a) We will suffer regardless, so why not make a virtue of necessity?
b) Suffering does occupy attention, and humans are easily bored.
c) Suffering exists and thus invites excuse, and people prefer absurd
    explanation to no explanation at all.
d) It just be that way, and thinking about it makes it feel worse.

Lonesome Booze Blues

If your answer was d), see me after the show.
If you picked any other answer, you are abandoned
to your own ideas and to the words wherewith
to think them, the clothes in which to lay them out.
Still, as minds are many, many are like, and say ours are ...
what say we hit the bars and hum a few bars together?
Come here, Mama, bring me a can of that lonesome booze.
Everything old gwine be young again someday, or ain't you heard
    the news?

Schlimmbesserung

One thing they could all agree on, it was going to get worse before it got better. The dealbreaker was whether outright catastrophe was any cause for celebration.

There were some who sang sweetly while swamp water dripped from their noses, harmonizing about how compost piles could soon be put away for good.

There were others who peered out as on a gathering of draft riots, sequestering their quality time behind a barricade of legal objections.

Certain ones rebuilt the storied cities, that these might be freshly destroyed. The radiant avenues looked wide as rivers, the spires appeared recycled from the architecture of amusement parks.

Certain others made preparations to absquatulate at need, getting their forged documents in order, sewing the numbers of anonymous bank accounts into the lining of their carefully casual clothes.

Some hankered to go upstairs right now dressed in nightshirts and party hats.

Some preferred to go upstairs with Margery. Others went up with Kate. Others went up there with the two of them together.

The most secure were most irate. They shouted and shouted down; they threw buckets of blood; they beat their kids the way it used to be done in the old days, before that art was lost.

The merely irritable had reached an age at which they were no longer certain of anything. Their children called them fools to their faces and disposed of their disposable income.

Some remained staunch individualists and were against socialized medicine. They visited the sick with satisfaction and held vast fleets of mobile homes in common.

Some wore negligées to charity balls. They were surprised to learn their husbands had decided to spend more time with their families.

Some were too clever by half. Some by perhaps a quarter. Some solved their problems with home-schooled math, addition

Schlimmbesserung

    by subtraction.
All sides believed that the others were ahead and that the stakes had never been so high. They accused reporters of distorting their positions, and about this they were of course right.
All pointed proudly to the proof found in their pudding, but that confection was never quite ready to eat. The sticky business of a dénouement was rescheduled for the following day.
In the interim, each sought armor in the truth. While the light held, the fight was joined, and the ground grew grumous.
Night fell as predicted in the manuals. More evil auguries were observed. A ruthless chiseling picked itself up and soldiered on into the gloom.

Teaching the Controversy

The police can always exist in a purer form.
Do not mention the unmentionable without crouching.
Do not depilate until told.
The right hand is better, but the left hand has more fun.
The Piercing Hut is available to all, but not all mutilations are
    equal.
Clothing matters.
Some wear underwear for protection, but I'm OK with a hat.
Certain tribes insist on sheaths, others prefer cocks unquivered.
Diet is important, and a low-salt diet is best.
Envy comes early to court.
Many are the lying motherfuckers.
Sex is important, and a low-salt diet is best.
It's three to get ready and four to adore, but numbers are all the
    same to me.
There is an art to violence, yea a season unto disemboweling.
Borrowing isn't stealing until you try it.
Raping women the wrong way is likely to cause bad feeling.
It's my story and meant every word it said.
You don't like it, you can kiss my cow.

Response

Out of the sky's abyss and from the depths of our solitude came our answered prayers.
They took their time coming, suspecting a trap.
Their vehicles were beyond all conception: narrow as phone-poles, longer than freight trains, blinding in motion as flashes of light.
Visually acute bipeds with distinct digits, they did not appear so odd as we had imagined. Struck by our strength, they were amazed by our simplicity.
They rarely ate us unless they were hungry. Their voyages were long, and we learned to avoid them on arrival.
They had no need to learn our language; our children learned theirs. Our grandchildren ceased to speak our own.
We had displayed ourselves male and female, and they enjoyed watching us mate. In this their amusement outstripped ours, and we often, exhausted, collapsed.
We had proffered our music, which pleased them, though they had trouble distinguishing pitch. Persons of whom song was required made melody or discord as ability and good grace allowed.
The Louvre was rescued from us and shipped off. Oceans were needed elsewhere.
They had many names for us, none complimentary. The least insulting was "those-who-say-hi-in-the-void."
If they sickened on contact with us, we did not know it. They were countless as the stars from which they came, and their numbers seemed never to decrease.
We, however, proved delicate, so that many of us died without seeing them, ill with mysterious ailments. Parasites hatched in our eyes, our skin turned to paste and smudged off, blood burst from our nose, our anus.
Occasionally they succeeded in impregnating us, though few of the offspring survived. Those that did became the future, earth's inheritors, a race horrible to behold.
Their religion was soon ours, our god in their image. Such stern theology was not unfamiliar, for if its benefits were abstract,

Response

    our sacrifice was real.
Spiral galaxy, nine planets, third world from its sun: we had sent our capsule into space the instant we were able, bearing its diagram of our position. Thus the word "NASA" became anathema, "probe" a term of abuse.
That our ideas be heeded, our suffering seen, in desperation we had announced ourselves, imploring the attention of time and distance, asking anything but to be alone and sufficient unto this day.

Event Horizon

There exists a verge beyond which we
can't know, a vastness past all gathered
evidence, exterior to our understanding,
space placed in excess of what place we see,

and whatever may obtain beyond the rift
dividing the perceived from the imagined
is speculation and suspect, its any instance
anonymous anomaly, its fact an uncaught drift,

and so delimited are all things under a sun.
Of course our areas of ignorance are various
in extent, ill envisioned zones of indeterminate
shape wherein idea and catastrophe are one.

Someday soon, when the planets are aligned
for good and migratory stars refill their nest,
a world will turn unseen, its restless moon
cease streaming beams as all its rays rewind.

The point where detectable energy disappears
in gravitation is a black hole's event horizon.
The closest such horizon in space is ages away;
my own, perhaps as much as thirty years.

Problems in Carolingian Art

If things can last, at length they simply exist
Beyond good or bad, complete in themselves,
The way oldest friends, when you see them again,
Needn't be smart or entertaining or even very nice,
They only have to remind you of the past you shared
And the way you felt in a previous incarnation,
Back when just having a future was enough;
The way Carolingian artifacts – call them art,
What the hell, rudimentary figurines standing
In time and type halfway between Cycladic stones
And Giacometti – get praised for their primitive vigor,
Their frank vitality, even if what they really are
Is awkward evidence, proof of an impoverished age,
The stick-figure record of a disastrous dumbing-down
To a level of sophistication far below that of Lascaux,
Fifteen millennia earlier and lightyears ahead....
Still, if Charlemagne – that sentimentalist who wished
Not only to restore an empire but also to rebuild
An aesthetic – could content himself with such stuff,
Why should we complain, it's one style among many,
And the point is, these figures live to tell of ancient days,
Waiting behind glass for us to pay passing attention
Out of boredom, loneliness, our limited ideas.
Yes, but why did they live on? How? What wand
Was waved that such incompetence was rewarded,
Carried forward to be collectible, salvaged to become
Conversation pieces, elevated to museum-shop chic?
It seems things set aside cannot escape that aura;
Made once to signify, they must ever keep it up,
And year by year more import casually accretes,
The intellectual, or just the emotional, equivalent
Of a patina the touch of many hands creates,
Although we would doubtless value their testimony
Even in the absence of perceived intention, and though
Their persisting is admittedly dependent on chance

Problems in Carolingian Art

(One tomb, pregnant with gold, goes unnoticed by thieves,
One manuscript – *Beowulf* – is rescued from the fire):
Sheer chance, freak caprice, unruly accident, and yet
Grant this, they were tough enough to take advantage
Of the luck that came their way, and we in our turn,
Casting about for objects to attach our meaning to,
May do worse than to recall such stubborn shapes,
These rachitic warriors, these spavined horses,
Twisted bits of bronze forged solid to their core,
Fashioned to endure and here and there endowed
With some small surprise, the odd detail
That animates, the mnemonic device of charm.

De Monumentis

"regalique situ pyramidum altius"

Bronze, schmonze, you want permanent,
build a pyramid, and Lord knows I try,
though admittedly in unorthodox fashion
and with anything but Pharaonic efficiency.
The results have not been pretty, although
I like to think they're prettier than they look,
that each of them is beautiful in its own way,
that they all bear some witness to this world,
that if people only got to know them ...
so passes another attempt at self criticism,
the γνωθι σεαυτων calling it, once more, a day,
detached evaluation prorogued to the morrow morn,
that routine bushwhacking wherein all compositional
difficulties will again be gathered, fiendish as ever.
The problem remains one of organization, really,
getting your captive Hebrews straightened away
a snap compared to ordering the sparks that flee
onward and upward from the bonfire of thought,
a logistical nightmare, too many to include them all,
and if only some, then who, what, when, and where,
and is any of it truly material? Speaking of which,
ageless materials just aren't what they used to be,
cyclopean block lately become a fissionable thing,
myth left out in the rain now shrunk to fairy tale,
and as for this rat's nest of crude contingencies,
the corralled ephemera with which we build,
let's not even go there, we found marmoreal cities
and left them styrofoam. In such midst it appears
we artless artisans have been the more deceived,
for when all else failed, and we tried in good faith
to say whatever it was we meant, the words
that had befriended us and promised paradise,
that held our hand these umpteen thousand years,
crumbled in our mouths like sweetmeats made of dust,
leaving us in separate lurches gripped each by an urge

De Monumentis

to improvise our outcry upon the instant's spur.
Yet still we heap them up, the syllables, higher
than Hagia Sophia, and to tear them down again,
or simply to regard their implacable collapse,
let the chips fall where they may, will be
someone else's job, his toy, his dream,
the conjugation and other sexwork proceeding
until what persists is a dog-eared landscape,
a trap-door campagna of desuetudinous views,
tricky terrain where some must wobbly walk
and only the acknowledged sun shine on.

Entry Level Elective

My first thought was he lied in every word
when he said not to bother making allusions
because editorial assistants are just not looking
for the sensation they have missed something –
nobody likes feeling stupid – and anyway all that
is over and done with now. But on second thought
(a thing he marked off for), I saw he was right:
the past is, by definition, *passé*, and what passes
for humanity here is human interest, the tears in
the parking lot, the singles bar pick-up returned
to the wild, the ornament resembling prison tattoos.

Do you have any addictions you would like to share?
Not so as I've noticed, but I'm willing to learn.
Describe your emotional weather in under ten words.
Willful ignorance is the global warming of the mind.

What It Takes

It takes so much to make a poem even a small and faithful one
bucolic quatrain stoic epitaph haiku's reticent gesture
it takes entire planets whole solar systems the vast peculiar
    cosmos of a carefully prepared understanding

Let's admit it poetry is not very efficient the genuine article
    demands all the light one mind can absorb to release such
    astonishing force
it asks every atom of our being to detonate the private Hiroshima
    of insight the half-life of lingering implication
poetry is destructive yes it has split more than one planet in two
    and yet it yields no more than the energy of which it is
    composed

Poetry demands a lot and the contents of a poem are not
    economical either
to describe even a glass of water necessitates several oceans
to observe so much as a hillock a knoll a rise requires an
    enormous range Carpathians the Hindu Kush and surely
    Shelley scaled many peaks getting a grip on Mont Blanc
what endless rivers flowed when Stevens gazed across the fateful
    one that runs past Haddam Meadows
how many soldiers died as Homer cut his hero down in dust

Poetry asks everything
it asks all the poems that have ever been all the people and places
    things and thoughts
poetry is to seek everywhere to find in any object no detail too
    cunning for it no elaboration too grandiose
it appears profligate
it shows itself multitudinous
it looks to overlap infinity or so it seems to the man at his
    keyboard each morning struggling to assemble materials
poetry wants whole worlds

What It Takes

But in fact it's not that easy
there exists just one world really and in it just several poets and in them only a very few poems

The Future of the Past

Bottom line, it doesn't have one;
or if it does, it's for the souvenir value,
a knickknack marketed under ghastly light
in the stale air of an outlet mall stretching
from here to eternity somewhere in Minnesota.
That's where yesterday will be made available,
shiny as today, where tomorrow's children
won't be doomed to repeat anything,
because it doesn't count as repeating if no one
ever finds out what happened the first time;
where they won't weep to discover much,
much less that Socrates has covered his face;
and where, standing on the shoulders of pygmies,
they'll see all the way to the far end
of the shopping center and the cinema now
showing a torrid, uplifting new love story
with a feel-good conclusion called *Anna Karenina*.
Freed from the maze of collective memory, children
need never confront minotaurs of self-recognition;
they'll have no use for the filament of philology,
won't abandon conscience on the shore of any island,
nor cause loved ones to leap into seas of despair, or
if they do, innocent is what they'll surely be found.
Protected so, they needn't grasp that people once
tried learning from the past and didn't enjoy
how it grew lonely without God in the attic
and awkward assembling an encyclopaedic
awareness of instances adding up to accident.
Lacking such perspective, they'll have no vantage
outside themselves and thus won't be forced
to face our era's essential anagnorisis,
i.e., to comprehend their unknowing
as a refuge sought, as a great migration,
a tribal return to the big-hearted homeland,
to the comfort that lies in the proximate

The Future of the Past

and the solace arriving on snow-white wings....
Well, such motion forms a current deep and wide,
and it didn't swim here to be dissuaded; besides,
look at it one way, and it's beautiful, really:
a pristine state of repaired awareness,
a new Eden all set up for new lapses,
another Renaissance in the making, though we,
of course, won't live to see that dawn; beautiful.
And meanwhile? Let's fold what light we can
into our words and set their volume on the shelf
to illuminate some hour as time and tide resolve.
No call to be sad about the ignorance, or mad, or
even worried. It's the Middle Ages, boys and girls.
We're the monks.

The Decline of the Western

It was in my early adolescence that the myth
of American masculinity changed, as the inarticulate
essentially justified loner defending Anglo-Saxon
society at the edge of civilization yielded place
to the argot-inflected essentially antinomian member
of an unAnglo-Saxon society bent on corrupting
civilization from within, or at least from New Jersey.
What I mean is, *Shane* gave way to *The Godfather*.
It is tempting to read something into this, though
in general I am suspicious of such undertakings
(the substitution of pop culture for what was once
called high culture being in my view not so much
the mark of democracy as a symptom of despair,
a sign high culture is no longer thought possible),
and I read into it that, when I was a teenager,
my country collectively became a teenager too,
sullenly disillusioned, psychologically bruised,
slouch-shouldered, acne-afflicted, snider than snot.
Reasons for this development, our Awkward Age,
are not far to seek, newly apprised as we all were
of the chasm isolating aspiration from event,
the self-mockery inherent in each good intention,
and maybe it was Viet Nam and Nixon that made
this nation suddenly more cynical than Diogenes,
or maybe it's a phase any political entity born
of high-minded rhetoric and dissembled compromise
inevitably arrives at, but there we were, America
and I, angry and depressed at the same time.
Since then, the two of us have been struggling
to mature in the absence of shared understanding
or accepted codes of conduct, and O my beloved,
beautiful, staggeringly stupid country, what madness
I have waded through with you, what enthusiasms,
enthrallments, what deranged quests for conviction.
There are days I swear we are fated to remain

The Decline of the Western

irremediable juveniles forever, but in time
we may yet achieve a moderate wisdom
(though I recognize our track record in this
regard is not good), may get the knack of masking
disappointment with the deadpan of adult demeanor
and muddle our way to the composure of a middle age
immune to wild schemes and purist extremes,
trading macrobiotic diets and flapdoodle religions
for solving crossword puzzles together and watching
old-time movies when they show up again on TV.
For my part, I still like westerns and prefer them
to mafia flicks, even if most of them are not
very well acted or much like frontier existence
(the clothes just aren't grubby or the women ugly
enough to simulate Dry Gulch convincingly).
I recognize this for sentimentality, but I find
the cinematic slaughter of swarthy Caucasians
posing as Amerindians somehow comforting.
I suppose, however self-serving or genocidal,
what appeals is the faint echo of heroic ideal.
When I was a child, I behaved and I spoke
like what I was, but coming to man's estate
I buried an idea of myself and my best
thoughts in the back yard with the dog.

The Prophet Joel on the Division of Labor

It is written *your young men shall see visions,*
And what else should they see,
Swept by flood tides of futurity
To irrational extremes
Of foresight; *your old men shall dream dreams,*
For which redundancy,
Those variously elaborated evasions
Of memory and art, it seems
They have been at last provided reasons.

Coup de Vieux

for Jasmin Trembley

Protected by landscape, its stand of mature
spruce draped in a blur of needles fine
as fabric deflecting both sunshine
and the view, and by the spreading stain
whose slow advance has come to constitute your

degenerative eyesight, only as kept
in mind does the nearby market town
stand beside the inland sea the Rhône
forms at Lac Leman. Two arcs of stone
jetty do not embrace the harbor except

as you picture them; yachts tied up to the quay
like galleys – so we may imagine,
here was a Roman port – at certain
hours present a half-lit illusion
of bustle and cast off lines to the degree

you consent; the dilapidated Château,
hôtel de ville for a rich terrain
and frugal populace, has each quoin
repointed, its face made up again
in plaster and paint, just as you choose to know

of it; and an antique paddle-wheel ferry
declines its scheduled civic mission
of stitching recollected vision
to the steep immediate mountain
on the farther shore, refusing to carry

anyone across, until you are willing
it be done. You think to let it run,
even if you can't abide the *bain*
that will be its object: Evian,
where those with liver complaints and like failing

Coup de Vieux

go to get well. Guests must be taking the cure
there now, attending each other's tone,
drinking their health, complimenting one
another's progress; and yet what can
the progress finally be that one must endure

year after year? On your side of the transport,
one passes time helped by the unseen
staff, fielding calls from what friends remain
and those anxious relations who mean
well and to visit. Given some last resort

is wanted, you elect three efficient rooms
defined on one hand by the curtain
drawn on a prospect that pales at dawn,
on the other by a door within
whence an anodyne arrives when night resumes.

Liturgy

Who comes now to this place?
A child. His sailor-suit is unsoiled, and his smile is as the sunlight in which he plays.
I don't know him. Here even the sun is dark, and clothing is not permitted. Who is it that has come?
A boy whose chores are done. He has fed the geese and fetched the milk and wishes to row upon the pond till supper.
I do not know him. To cross these waters is no pastime, and no meal waits. Again, who comes to this place?
A striving lad. There are scraps of Latin in his mouth, and he practices striking a ball. He is beautiful, if only when he thinks himself unseen.
I tell you I don't know him. Practice is superfluous here. We have plenty of beauty and Latin, too, and neither is wanted. Who is it you say has come?
A man grown to his vigor. He can swim distances, he can dance into the night, he cannot exhaust his strength. See, he requires little light to read and takes easily to sleep.
But I don't know him. Here is less light than that, and sleep holds no interest. Who comes this way?
A man in the eyes of others. His hands have learned their skill, he has a head for facts, he knows his mind and has conceived his aim.
I know no such man. The men I am acquainted with never learn, and they are forever aiming at nothing. In any case, no fact obtains here or skill avails. Who has come?
A man arrived at wisdom. His shoulder aches always, and even his pubic hair is gray. He owns property, and people ask his opinion, though they listen as little as ever.
And yet I don't know him. I hear many opinions, and they distinguish nobody. Tell me, who comes?
A creature stogged in age. He has abandoned his memories and kept only his smile. It is childlike, right to the missing teeth.
Still I don't think I know him. Here age is all one, and teeth are scattered liberally. I ask you, who is it that comes now to be

Liturgy

buried in this place?
A dwindled image, a shape of sorrow, a figuration of dust. The man appears as you have always known him.
Then let him in. Let the image lie down. Let it lose its shape and keep its peace. As it has been before, so may it be again.

Life and Death Matters

Well, it's what we have to work with, anyhow,
and hard it is not to feel there must be an answer
when there is so evidently a problem.
I saw the grimace set on my mother's lips,
and I kissed that waxen brow, and what
other scene shall come to me
when my hands fall idle now? Turn
and turn it, the edge grows no easier to grasp,
which is why any twelve-step program
worthy of the name insists you place
final responsibility for the weight of the world
in someone else's hands, preferably God's,
and while for the purpose of Federal funding
theological details are left to individual discretion,
still the pressure is heavy to stop thinking
if you seriously wish to stop drinking,
or gambling, rambling, staying
out late at night, or any of our inventive
resorts to the short-circuit – if it felt good we did it,
if not, we tried something else – so that even
the elaborate ratiocinations of Aquinas at last
boil down to faith, that is, to an abdication,
to junk the whole process and jump,
as if analysis unexercised could ever be content.
It seems the best advice of revealed wisdom
is simply to sit tight and shut up, but you
can tell it to the Marines, tell it to any order,
for how not to be distracted by the pilfered spark
that sputters through our dim wayfaring?
What is this talent that it should be set aside,
a sacrifice to grandeur, be left to wither,
a caduke deodand, vestigial sense,
the one gift that was ours besides tolerance
for pain and the brute instinct to endure?
A small power and a large misunderstanding,

Life and Death Matters

a hope chest made to furnish mansions,
the humble service laid in banquet halls,
the home-made drapes too short, that's what;
and if apprehension be a cottage dower,
predicament vast estate, why then the plot
we're told to tend is too extensive for our tools,
our little pail and shovel and shears, and we
will never get clear of this corrupt garden,
there is no angel to show us the door,
but must wander in amazement till we lie down
in dismay, and does the meantime matter?
It matters, though not in disbelief's suspension.
It matters, it matters, but as a garment does,
a weave to wear, not some web to brush aside,
as the act of seeing matters, not the haze to be
seen through, matters just as thought
itself, now the solvent, now the solute,
never the solution.

A Note About George Bradley

George Bradley was born in Roslyn, New York, in 1953 and was educated at Yale University and the University of Virginia. Among the awards his work has received are the Witter Bynner Prize from the American Academy and Institute of Arts and Letters, a grant from the National Endowment for the Humanities, and the Yale Younger Poets Prize (1985, judge James Merrill).

Besides writing books, Bradley has been occupied in many ways – as a construction worker (installing foam insulation), as a copywriter (on staff at several small advertising companies in New York City), as a sommelier (at The American Hotel in Sag Harbor, Long Island, a restaurant with 650 wines on the list, 15,000 bottles in the cellar, and vintages going back to the 1800s), and as an editor (cleaning up translations from the Japanese for the Jack Tilton art gallery). Like most poets, he has also taught creative writing on occasion. Currently he imports and distributes La Bontà di Fiesole, a brand of olive oil made from the seven hundred trees on a family farm outside Florence and described by him as "the elixir of life." When not on the farm, Bradley lives in Chester, Connecticut.

Other books from Waywiser

POETRY

Al Alvarez, *New & Selected Poems*
Robert Conquest, *Penultimata*
Morri Creech, *Field Knowledge*
Peter Dale, *One Another*
Erica Dawson, *Big-Eyed Afraid*
B. H. Fairchild, *The Art of the Lathe*
Jeffrey Harrison, *The Names of Things: New & Selected Poems*
Joseph Harrison, *Identity Theft*
Joseph Harrison, *Someone Else's Name*
Anthony Hecht, *Collected Later Poems*
Anthony Hecht, *The Darkness and the Light*
Carrie Jerrell, *After the Revival*
Rose Kelleher, *Bundle o' Tinder*
Matthew Ladd, *The Book of Emblems*
Dora Malech, *Shore Ordered Ocean*
Eric McHenry, *Potscrubber Lullabies*
Timothy Murphy, *Very Far North*
Ian Parks, *Shell Island*
Chris Preddle: *Cattle Console Him*
Christopher Ricks, ed. *Joining Music with Reason:
34 Poets, British and American, Oxford 2004-2009*
Daniel Ritenburgh, *Advent*
W.D. Snodgrass: *Not for Specialists: New & Selected Poems*
Mark Strand, *Blizzard of One*
Bradford Gray Telford, *Perfect Hurt*
Cody Walker, *Shuffle and Breakdown*
Deborah Warren, *The Size of Happiness*
Clive Watkins, *Jigsaw*
Richard Wilbur, *Mayflies*
Richard Wilbur, *Collected Poems 1943-2004*
Norman Williams, *One Unblinking Eye*
Greg Williamson, *A Most Marvelous Piece of Luck*

FICTION

Gregory Heath, *The Entire Animal*
Matthew Yorke, *Chancing It*

ILLUSTRATED

Nicholas Garland, *I wish ...*

NON-FICTION

Neil Berry, *Articles of Faith: The Story of British Intellectual Journalism*
Mark Ford, *A Driftwood Altar: Essays and Reviews*
Richard Wollheim, *Germs: A Memoir of Childhood*